Talk to Me 3

2ND Edition

Happy House

Contents

Picture Description

Picture Discussion

Talk to Me 3

Story Making

Debate

Syllabus

Unit	Title	Talking About	Example
01	That Doesn't Belong	groups of things	• The bird has two legs. The pig, horse, and sheep all have four legs. The bird can fly, but the other animals can't fly.
02	This Is Heavier	comparing two things or people	• The backpack is heavier than the balloon. The backpack is lighter than the elephant.
03	Who Is the Youngest?	comparing more than two things or people	• The girl is the youngest. The alligator is the most dangerous.
04	The Light Is on in the House	pictures	• There is a house, a river, and tall green trees. Some birds are flying in the sky. It looks like it might rain. It looks peaceful.
05	That's Not Right!	things that are wrong	• There are some flowers on the clouds. They should be in the garden. There are carrots in the tree. They should be underground.
06	What Is Similar and Different?	similarities and differences	• They are having a class. The boys are in the classroom. The girls are at the gym. The boys are not wearing uniforms. The girls are wearing sports uniforms.
07	How Often Do You Eat Out?	frequency	• I eat fast food once a week. • I never eat fast food.
08	What Is He Going to Do?	predictions	• The boy is going to paint a picture because he has a paintbrush, paper, and paint. • The boy has a paintbrush, paper, and paint, so he is going to paint a picture.

Unit	Title	Talking About	Example
09	When Do You Yawn?	certain times	• I yawn when I'm bored. • When I'm sleepy, I yawn.
10	Let's Make Plans!	plans	• After school, we will ride bikes to the park. We will play tag there.
11	I Would Do If I Could Do	possible situations	• I would swim at the beach because it is a hot day. • I would ride on a rollercoaster because it is exciting.
12	We Had a Good Time	the past	• Last week, I went to an Italian restaurant for my mom's birthday. We ate pizza, pasta, and a birthday cake.
13	Ask Me a Question!	asking questions	• What are they doing? Why are they standing at the door?
14	Tell Me a Story!	retelling stories	• In the beginning, the witch gave an apple to Snow White. In the middle, Snow White ate the apple. In the end, Snow White fell asleep.
15	What Do You Think?	opinions	• I think so too because I can wake up early the next day. • I don't think so because I want to play more.
16	What Should Children Do?	opinions	• I agree because we can get fresh air. • I disagree because I don't like playing sports.

How to Use This Book

This section is an introduction to the unit and grabs the attention of the students. It has a focus picture followed by three questions. The questions are either comprehension or conversational and are designed to get students talking straight away. Some of the questions act as a springboard to the rest of the unit.

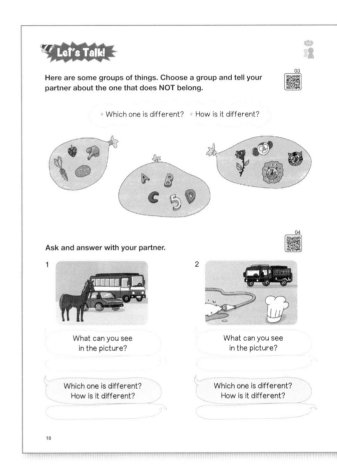

You Can Say This

This part is directly related to some of the questions above. It gives the students key or example phrases and sentences used throughout the unit.

Let's Talk!

This section has two parts. The first part is designed as a conversation. It is a fun way for the students to answer a specific question as they may choose one or two answers from a selection of several choices. The second part allows the students to look at mini pictures and answer questions checking their comprehension and giving them a chance to speak.

Picture Bingo

Work in pairs. Take turns saying what you see in the picture and how it makes you feel. Find and say the number of the picture your partner is talking about. Circle the pictures you and your partner chose. The winner is the first one who has four circles in a row and calls out, "Bingo!"

Player 1

Player 2 goes to page 84.

24

Odd One Out!

Work in pairs. Find the odd one out in each line as fast as you can and tell your partner. The winner is the one who finds the most.

12

Speak Out!

Choose one group and say which one in the group is different and how.

1

2

Unit 1 That Doesn't Belong 11

Speak Out!

This section is a group or class activity. It has one question and two large pictures. Each of the pictures has enough material for groups to generate different answers.

Fun Activities

This section allows the students to reinforce or expand their speaking in a fun way. Each unit has activities such as bingo, spot the differences, information gap, find a friend, and a board game. The students can relax and have fun while using English.

✦ Review Test · Teaching Materials
free download at www.ihappyhouse.co.kr

That Doesn't Belong

01

Look and talk.

1 What can you see in the picture?

2 What are all these things?

3 Which one is different? How is it different?

02

 **You Can Say This**

• when talking about groups of things

The bird has two legs.
The pig, horse, and sheep all have four legs.
The bird can fly, but the other animals can't fly.

03

Here are some groups of things. Choose a group and tell your partner about the one that does NOT belong.

☆ Which one is different? ☆ How is it different?

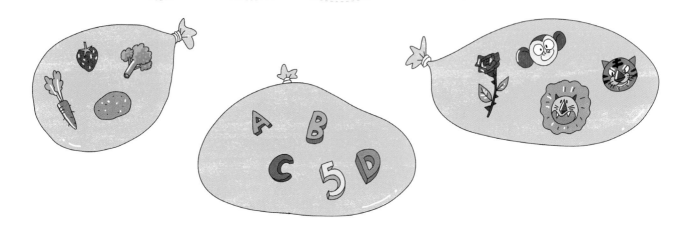

04

Ask and answer with your partner.

1

What can you see
in the picture?

Which one is different?
How is it different?

2

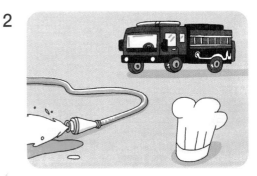

What can you see
in the picture?

Which one is different?
How is it different?

Choose one group and say which one in the group is different and how.

1

2

Odd One Out!

Work in pairs. Find the odd one out in each line as fast as you can and tell your partner. The winner is the one who finds the most.

Unit 02 This Is Heavier

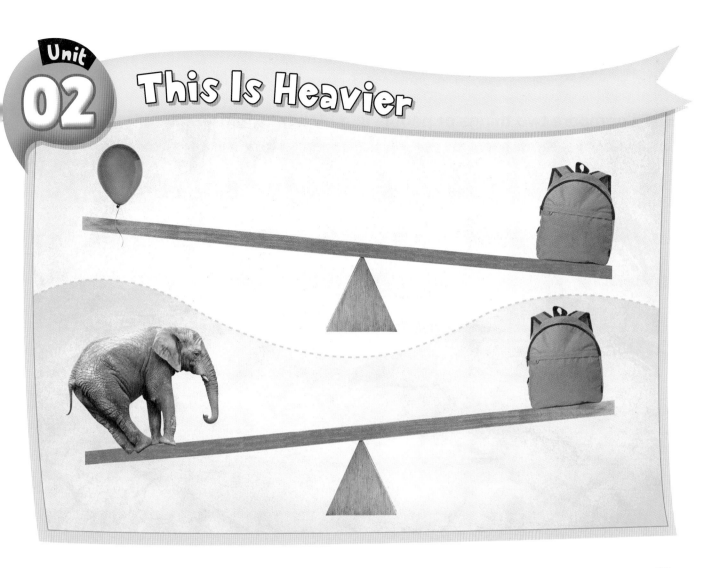

05

Look and talk.

1 What can you see in the picture?

2 Which is heavier, the balloon or the backpack?

3 Is the backpack heavier than the elephant?

06

 **You Can Say This**

• when comparing two things or people

> The backpack is heavier than the balloon.
> The backpack is lighter than the elephant.

Let's compare two things or people in a picture! Choose and tell your partner about them by using the words below.

✳ Which one is smaller? ✳ Who is faster?

big / small

fast / slow

strong / weak

fat / thin

Ask and answer with your partner.

1

Which dress is longer?

Which dress is more expensive?

2

Which place is louder?

What other places are louder than the library?

Speak Out!

In the first picture, say what is scarier for the girl and talk about yourself. In the second picture, say what is more exciting for the boy and talk about yourself.

Let's Compare!

Flip a coin and move along the board. When you land on each space, compare the things or people by using the given word.

+1   +2

Start
dirty
bright
high
long
beautiful
slow
young
short
big
hot
soft
tall
thick
Finish

Who Is the Youngest?

Look and talk.

1 What can you see in the picture?

2 Who is the oldest and the youngest in the family?

3 Which is the most dangerous animal in the zoo?

 You Can Say This

• when comparing more than two things or people

The grandfather is the oldest.
The girl is the youngest.
The alligator is the most dangerous.

You can be the best at something. Choose and talk with your partner.

✧ What do you want to be the best at?

Ask and answer with your partner.

1

Which animal is the tallest?

Who is the tallest
in your family?

2

Canada

USA

Mexico

Which country is the biggest?

Which is the biggest city
in our country? What do you
think about the city?

 **Speak Out!**

Talk about what is happening and how the boy or girl feels. Then, talk about your happiest or saddest day.

1

2

Who is the Fastest?

Flip a coin and move along the board. When you land on each space, answer the question in a full sentence.

+1   +2

Start

What is the funniest movie you have seen?

Who is the tallest boy in the class? How tall is he?

Who is the tallest girl in the class? How tall is she?

What is the most delicious food? When did you eat it?

Who is the best singer? What is your favorite song?

What is the most difficult school subject for you?

Who has the biggest bag in the class?

What is the most fun thing to do at the park?

Whose hair is the longest in the class?

What is the heaviest thing in your bag?

What is the biggest animal in the ocean?

Finish

13

Look and talk.

1 What can you see in the picture?

2 What is the weather like in the picture?

3 How does the picture make you feel?

14

 You Can Say This   • when talking about pictures

> There is a house, a river, and tall green trees.
> Some birds are flying in the sky.
> Some birds are in the river and on the grass.
> It looks like it might rain. It looks peaceful.

 **Let's Talk!**

Here are some beautiful places to visit. Choose your favorite one and tell your partner about it.

> ✫ What does the place look like?

Ask and answer with your partner.

1

> Who can you see in the picture?

>

> What is the astronaut doing?

>

2

> What can you see in the picture?

>

> What feeling do you get from the picture?

>

Speak Out!

Say what you can see. Then, talk about how you feel about the pictures.

1

2

Picture Bingo

Work in pairs. Take turns saying what you see in the picture and how it makes you feel. Find and say the number of the picture your partner is talking about. Circle the pictures you and your partner chose. The winner is the first one who has four circles in a row and calls out, "Bingo!"

Player 1

Player 2 goes to page 86.

That's Not Right!

Look and talk.

17

1 Where are the flowers?

2 Where should the flowers be?

3 What other things are wrong with the picture?

18

 **You Can Say This**

• when talking about things that are wrong

> There are some flowers on the clouds.
> They should be in the garden.
> There are carrots in the tree. They should be underground.
> The roof is on the grass. It should be on the house.

Let's Talk!

Something is wrong with the pictures. Choose and tell your partner about it.

✶ What is wrong with the picture?

Ask and answer with your partner.

1

Who is there in the kitchen?

What else is wrong with the picture?

2

What is wrong with the picture?

Where should the boat be?

Say what is wrong with the pictures.

1

2

Strange World

Flip a coin and move along the board. When you land on each space, say what is wrong with the picture.

+1 +2

What Is Similar and Different?

21

Look and talk.

1 What are the people in the pictures doing?

2 Where are they?

3 What are they wearing?

You Can Say This • when talking about how things are similar and different

There are teachers and students. They are having a class.
The boys are in the classroom. The girls are at the gym.
The boys are not wearing uniforms.
The girls are wearing sports uniforms.

Here are the four seasons. Choose two seasons and ask your partner about the differences between them.

✩ What are the differences between the two seasons?

Ask and answer with your partner.

1

What is similar
about the people?

What differences
can you find?

2

What is similar
about the houses?

What differences
can you find?

Talk about the similarities and differences of the pictures.

1

2

How Are They Similar or Different?

Work in pairs. In the first pictures, find the four similar things as fast as you can and tell your partner. In the second pictures, find the four different things as fast as you can and tell your partner. The winner is the one who says the most sentences.

1

2

How Often Do You Eat Out?

Look and talk.

1 What is happening in the picture?

2 Do you like fast food?

3 How often do you eat fast food?

You Can Say This • when talking about how often you do something

- I eat fast food every day.
- I eat fast food once a week.
- I eat fast food twice a month.
- I never eat fast food.

Here are the activities people often do. Choose and ask your partner.

☆ How often do you do this activity?

Ask and answer with your partner.

1

What are the people doing?

How often do you go to
the movie theater?
Who do you go with?

2

How often do you say
"I love you" to your parents?

What do your parents say
back to you?

Speak Out!

In the first picture, choose one place and say how often you visit and what you do there. In the second picture, choose one way to travel and say how often you travel with it and why you like it or not.

1

2

How Often Do You Do That?

Flip a coin and move along the board. When you land on each space, say how often you do the activity.

+1 +2

Start

watch TV

buy new clothes

eat chocolate

get up at 7 o'clock

go to bed after 11 o'clock

meet your friends after school

play computer games

Finish

play badminton

play the piano

eat fruits

listen to music

take a shower

What Is He Going to Do?

29

Look and talk.

1 Where is the boy in the picture?

2 What is he going to do?

3 Why do you think so?

30

 **You Can Say This** • when talking about the future based on what is happening

> • The boy is going to paint a picture because he has a paintbrush, paper, and paint.
> • The boy has a paintbrush, paper, and paint, so he is going to paint a picture.

Let's guess what someone is going to do! Choose and tell your partner.

31

* What is he/she going to do next?

32

Ask and answer with your partner.

1

What is happening
in the picture?

What is the girl going to do?

2

What is going to happen to
the woman's shopping bag?

Why do you think so?

Speak Out!

Choose one person and talk about what he or she is going to do.

1

2

What Are They Going to Do?

Flip a coin and move along the board. When you land on each space, say what the person or people are going to do.

+1 🪙 🪙 +2

Unit 09

When Do You Yawn?

33

Look and talk.

1 What is happening in the picture?

2 Why do you think the boy is yawning?

3 When do you usually yawn?

34

 You Can Say This   • when talking about when something happens

- I yawn when I'm tired.
- I yawn when I'm bored.
- When I'm sleepy, I yawn.

Let's Talk!

Here are some places around town. Choose and talk with your partner.

> ☆ When do you go to this place?

post office

bookstore

dentist's office

supermarket

Ask and answer with your partner.

1

> What is the girl doing?

> When do you water plants?

2

> What is the boy doing?

> When do you wear a helmet?

Speak Out!

Talk about what is happening and what you would say at that time.
Then, talk about when you say "I'm sorry" or "Thank you."

1

2

When Do You Do That?

Flip a coin and move along the board. When you land on each space, answer the question.

+1 🪙 🪙 +2

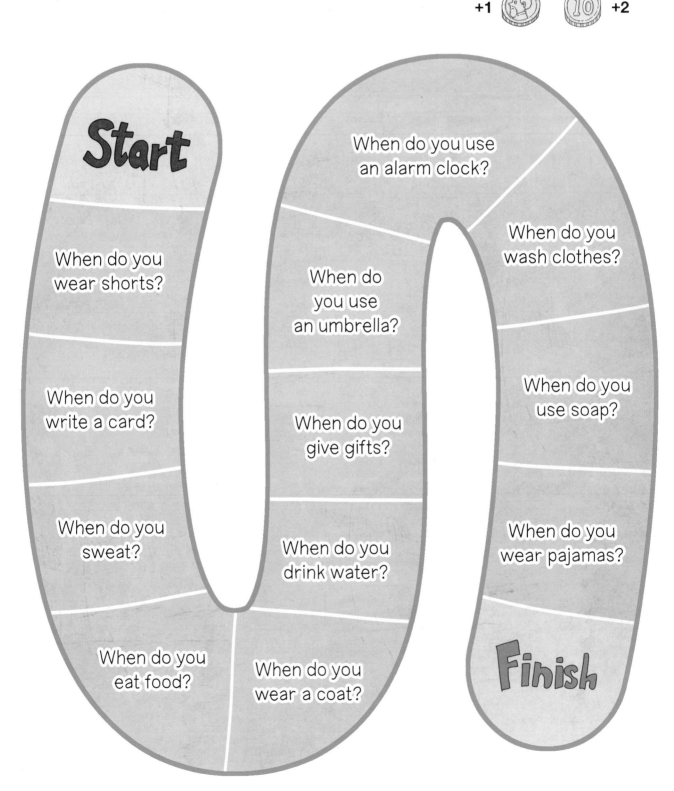

Start

When do you wear shorts?

When do you write a card?

When do you sweat?

When do you eat food?

When do you wear a coat?

When do you use an umbrella?

When do you give gifts?

When do you drink water?

When do you use an alarm clock?

When do you wash clothes?

When do you use soap?

When do you wear pajamas?

Finish

Let's Make Plans!

37

Look and talk.

1 Where will the children go after school? How will they get there?

2 What will they do there?

3 What will you do after school today?

38

 **You Can Say This**

• when talking about what you will do

> After school, we will ride bikes to the park.
> We will play tag there.

Let's Talk!

Imagine you are planning for this weekend. Choose a place and the way to travel and tell your partner.

> ✴ Where will you go this weekend?   ✴ How will you get there?

Ask and answer with your partner.

1

> What will the boy do
> with his money?

> Who will he go
> skateboarding with?

2

> When will the children
> go to the farm?

> What will they do there?

46

Speak Out!

Talk about the children's plans for a birthday party or field trip. Then, make your own plans with your classmates.

1

2

Find a Friend!

Circle your answer to each question and ask your classmates the questions. The winner is the first one who finds a friend with the same plan.

How to play

Q What will you do <u>this Saturday</u>?

A I'll <u>play badminton.</u> ➡ Write his/her name and ask the next question(Who will you do it with?).

A I'll <u>go bowling.</u> ➡ Ask another classmate.

This Saturday

What will you do?		
Who will you do it with?	my family my brother or sister my friends	
What time will you do it?	12:00 01:00 03:00	

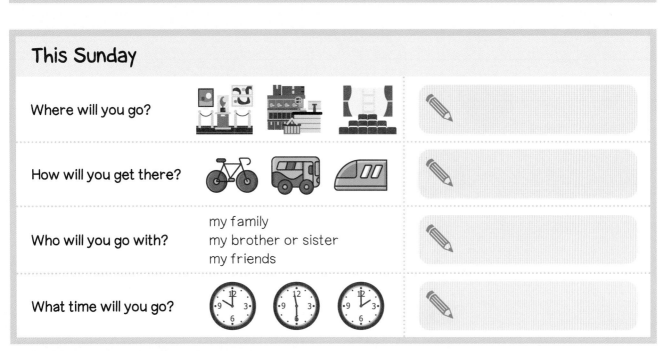

This Sunday

Where will you go?		
How will you get there?		
Who will you go with?	my family my brother or sister my friends	
What time will you go?		

I Would Do If I Could Do

Brian

Emma

Greg

41

Look and talk.

1 What do the children want to do?

2 Where should they go to do that?

3 If you could do something fun right now, what would you do? Why?

42

You Can Say This

• when talking about if you could do something

• I would swim at the beach because it is a hot day.

• I would ride on a rollercoaster because it is exciting.

• I would go to the zoo to see the kangaroos because they are my favorite animals.

43

Imagine you can have a job for one day. Choose and talk with your partner.

✷ Which job would you choose? Why?

44

Ask and answer with your partner.

1

What is the man doing?

If you could paint your bedroom, what color would you paint it? Why?

2

Why do you think they are wearing costumes?

If you could wear any Halloween costume, what would you wear? Why?

 **Speak Out!**

Say what you can see. Then, talk about if you would go there or not and give reasons.

1

2

If You Could

Flip a coin and move along the board. When you land on each space, answer the question and explain.

+1 +2

Start	If you could watch TV this afternoon, what would you watch?	If you could plan the school lunch menu for tomorrow, what would you choose?

If you could live anywhere, where would you live?

If you could meet any favorite actor, who would you meet?	If you could choose a new after-school class, what would it be?

If you could have a new pet, what would it be?

If you could design your own T-shirt, what would you choose?

Finish

If you could write a story, what would you write about?

If you could change your name, what would you choose?	If you could speak any languages, what would you choose?	If you could meet any favorite singer, who would you meet?	If you could buy new clothes today, what would you buy?

We Had a Good Time

Look and talk.

1 What are the family doing in the restaurant?

2 How did they get to the restaurant?

3 When was the last time you went to a restaurant? What did you eat?

45

 You Can Say This

• when talking about what happened in the past

46

Last week, I went to an Italian restaurant
for my mom's birthday. We went there by car.
We ate pizza, pasta, and a birthday cake.
We had a good time.

 **Let's Talk!**

47

Have you helped others? Choose what you did and tell your partner.

☆ When did you help someone?   ☆ What did you do?

48

Ask and answer with your partner.

1

What are the people doing?

When was the last time
you got new clothes?
What did you get?

2

What is the girl doing?

How did you feel when you
sang in front of people?
What did you sing?

Talk about what is happening and how the boy and girl feel. Then, talk about the last time you felt like him and her. Say when, where, why, and who you were with at that time.

1

2

Beat the Clock!

Ask your classmates the following questions. You can only ask a classmate one question. When someone answers the question, ask him or her to write their name on your chart. Ask as many different classmates as possible until the time is up. The winner is the one who has the most names.

When was the last time ...

... you had a cold?
What did you do?

... you ate a hamburger?
Where did you eat it?

... you met your grandparents?
What did you do?

... you went to the hospital?
How did you get there?

... you wrote a card?
Who was the card for?

... you took a lot of photos?
Where were you?

... you laughed so much?
What was so funny?

... you rode a bike?
Where did you go?

... you had a haircut?
Who did you go with?

Ask Me a Question!

49

Look and talk.

1 Where are the people in the picture?

2 Ask your teacher a question about the people, using *what*.

3 Ask your teacher a question about the people, using *why*.

50

 **You Can Say This**

• when asking questions

When is it?
Who are the people? Where are they?
What are they doing?
Why are they standing at the door?

Here are some activities we do every day. Choose and ask your partner about when he or she does that.

☆ When do you do that?

Ask and answer with your partner.

1

Where is the girl?

Ask your partner about
why the girl is crying.

2

What is the girl doing?

Ask your partner about
the girl or the dog, using *why*.

Speak Out!

Choose one item or place and ask a question about it, using *where*, *what*, or *when*. Your classmates will guess what you are talking about and answer the question.

1

2

• Learn About Jake and Lily! •

Work in pairs. Take turns asking questions, using the given word *where*, *when*, *what*, or *who*. Write your partner's answer to fill in the blank. The winner is the first pair to finish.

 Player 1

☞ Player 2 goes to page 87.

- I'm from _____ . (where)

- My birthday is _____ . (when)

- My favorite food is _____ . (what)

- My favorite singer is _____ . (who)

- Every Saturday, I _____ . (what)

- I want to be a _____ later. (what)

Jake

- I'm from England.

- My favorite season is spring.

- My favorite color is blue.

- My best friend is Tom.

- Every Sunday, I go to the library.

- I want to be a doctor later.

Lily

Look and talk.

1 Who can you see in the picture?

2 What happened in the beginning?

3 What happened in the middle and in the end?

 **You Can Say This**

• when retelling stories

In the beginning, the witch gave an apple to Snow White.
In the middle, Snow White ate the apple.
In the end, Snow White fell asleep.

Let's Talk!

Can you tell this story? Choose one part of the story and tell your partner.

✲ What happened in the beginning, in the middle, and in the end?

Ask and answer with your partner.

1 Put the numbers in order and tell the story in three parts: the beginning, the middle, and the end.

2 Why do you think the rabbit took a nap in the race?

Speak Out!

Tell the story by using the pictures. Then, tell the story again in three parts: the beginning, the middle, and the end.

Story Retelling

Make groups. Read each story and answer the questions together.
Then, share the story summary with your classmates as a group.

There was once a king. A man came to visit the king and showed him a coat. The man said, "Only very smart people can see this beautiful coat." The king could not see the coat, but he wanted to be smart. He said, "Oh, my! It is wonderful. Please make me some clothes." The man came back another day with the king's new clothes. The king could not see the clothes, but he put them on and then walked in a parade. A boy called out, "Look, the king has no clothes on!" Everyone laughed at the king.

1 What happened in the beginning?
2 What happened in the middle?
3 What happened in the end?

"I am the strongest." the sun said to the wind. "No, I am the strongest!" the wind said back. They saw a man walking below. The sun said, "If you can get him to take off his coat, you are the strongest. But if I can get him to take off his coat, then I am the strongest." The wind agreed. The wind tried first. The wind blew and blew. The man held on to his coat tight. The wind blew again, but the man kept his coat on. The sun had his turn. The sun shined brightly. Finally, the man took off his coat. The sun was the winner.

1 What happened in the beginning?
2 What happened in the middle?
3 What happened in the end?

What Do You Think?

59

Look and talk.

1 What is happening in the pictures?

2 Do you usually go to bed early or late?

3 Going to bed early is good. Do you agree?

60

 **You Can Say This**

• when talking about your opinions

• I think so too because I can wake up early the next day.
• I don't think so because I want to play more.

Which sport do you think is dangerous? Choose and ask your partner if he or she agrees.

☆ I think this sport is dangerous. Do you agree?

Ask and answer with your partner.

1 What is happening in the pictures?

2 Are zoos good for animals?

   Tell your partner what you think and ask if he or she agrees.

 **Speak Out!**

Say which statement you agree with and why. Write down the names of your classmates who are on the same side as you.

1

Having a brother or sister is great.

Vs.

Having a brother or sister is not good.

2

Being a celebrity would be great.

Vs.

Being a celebrity would not be good.

Let's Debate!

Read and debate.

How to debate

1 Read the statement and take a side.

2 Make teams with students who are on the same side.

3 Brainstorm reasons why you agree or disagree. Then, write them down.

4 Now, the debate begins! The two teams take turns saying one reason at a time. The winner is the team that has the most reasons.

Pets are great.

Agree

Disagree

Going hiking is great.

Agree

Disagree

What Should Children Do?

Look and talk.

1 What is happening in the picture?

2 Do you like to play outside?

3 Children should play outside every day. What do you think?

You Can Say This

• when talking about your opinions

• I agree because we can get fresh air.
• I think so because we need to run around.
• I disagree because I don't like playing sports.
• I don't think so because I like playing computer games.

 **Let's Talk!**

What should children do every day? Choose and ask your partner if he or she agrees.

> ✳ Children should do this everyday. Do you agree?

Ask and answer with your partner.

1 What is happening in the pictures?
2 Do you think children should have cellphones?

   Tell your partner what you think and ask if he or she agrees.

Say which statement you agree with and why. Write down the names of your classmates who are on the same side as you.

1

Children should help with chores at home.

Children should not help with chores at home.

2

Children should play computer games.

Children should not play computer games.

Let's Debate!

Read and debate.

Children should not eat junk food.

Agree

Disagree

Children should bring pets to school.

Agree

Disagree

Appendices

Key Words

Unit 01

leg

vegetables

fruit

letters

number

animals

flower

wheel

wing

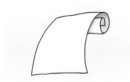
paper

float

brick

Unit 02

heavier

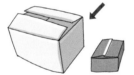
bigger

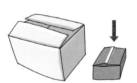
smaller

faster

slower

thinner

fatter

longer

more expensive

louder

vampire

ghost

Unit 03

zoo

the oldest

the youngest

panda

alligator

singing

playing basketball

drawing

cooking

the tallest

the biggest

have many birthday gifts

Unit 04

fly

look peaceful

lots of buildings

ride camels

mountain

big balloons

astronaut

look very cold

read a book to the daughter

teddy bear

lamp

curtain

Unit 05

ski at the beach

play soccer with a baseball

wear a coat

swim in a wedding dress

clown

bed

a man in a boat

nurse

tiger

tent

play the guitar

stand on the desk

Unit 06

have a class

sports uniform

blossom

leaves

made of wood

made of bricks

sheep

cow

angry

feed

hold an umbrella

buy ice cream

Unit 07

fast food restaurant

order

every day

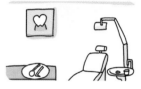

once a week

study

watch a movie

parents

go to the dentist

borrow books

park

train

airplane

Unit 08

paintbrush

letter

water

is going to fall asleep

banana peel

is going to snowboard

is going to skate

is going to fall down

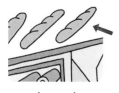

bread

is going to bake

is going to dry her hair

is going to rain

Unit 09

tired

yawn

sleepy

post office

bookstore

supermarket

water the plants

put on a helmet

broke a cup

give a gift

shorts

alarm clock

Unit 10

bike

play tag

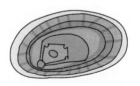
baseball stadium

museum

aquarium

skateboard

ride horses

4 o'clock

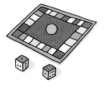
board game

Friday

lunch box

bowling

Unit 11

ride on a rollercoaster

kangaroo

actor

vet

race car driver

teacher

chef

paint

Halloween

rocket

penguins

seal

Unit 12

celebrate

helped my brother with his homework

carried her bag

lent a pencil to my friend

shop

happy

sad

scared

have a cold

write a card

laugh

have a haircut

take a shower

eat dinner

go to bed

watch TV

hospital

bathe the dog

spoon

nest

bakery

bathroom

school

socks

Unit 14

fell asleep

watch

followed the rabbit

smaller than the butterfly

turtle

race

took a nap

won the race

visit

chase

go to the city

king

Unit 15

wake up early

dangerous

bungee jumping

scuba diving

giraffes

brother

sister

fight

celebrity

debate

pet

going hiking

Unit 16

play outside

opinions

fresh air

play sports

eat vegetables

jump rope

cellphone

chores at home

play computer games

brainstorm

junk food

bring pets to school

Talk Some More 1

Roll a die and move along the board. Answer the questions or talk about the pictures.

big

If you could choose a place for your birthday party, where would you choose?

Talk about what you did yesterday.

How often do you clean your room?

slow

Miss a Turn

Ask a question, using *where*.

When do we wait in line?

What is the most difficult school subject?

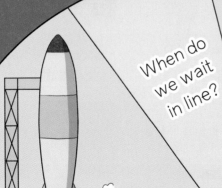

What doesn't belong?

Talk about your last birthday.

Start

82

What will you do this Sunday?

Stand Up Three Times

Going to an amusement park is great. Do you agree?

Finish

Go Back to START

Who is the funniest in the class?

What will you do after this class?

tall

Find a friend who ate a hamburger last week.

Students should have homework. Do you agree? Why or why not?

Ask a question, using *who*.

Roll the Die Again

When do you laugh?

How often do you watch TV?

Talk Some More 2

Roll a die and move along the board. Answer the questions or talk about the pictures.

Start!

What is the highest mountain in the country?

How often do you watch movies?

When do we take medicines?

fas

Wearing a school uniform is great. Why do you think so or not?

Ask a question, using *what*.

Miss A Turn

Find a friend who played soccer yesterday

If you could be at home alone for a day, what would you do?

What doesn't belong?

Talk about your last weekend.

What is the same?

Ta abo you fam

When do you say "Excuse me"?

Who is the youngest in your family?

Shout 'Hurray' Two Times

What is he going to do?

What is he going to do?

Ask a question, using *why*.

Move Ahead 2 SPACES

What is the easiest school subject?

How often do you have English class?

What doesn't belong?

5

...at is he going to do?

What will you do for your mom on Mother's Day?

What will you do after dinner?

If you could get some pocket money, what would you do with it?

Finish!

Picture Bingo

Work in pairs. Take turns saying what you see in the picture and how it makes you feel. Find and say the number of the picture your partner is talking about. Circle the pictures you and your partner chose. The winner is the first one who has four circles in a row and calls out, "Bingo!"

Player 2

Learn About Jake and Lily!

Work in pairs. Take turns asking a question, using the given word *where*, *when*, *what*, or *who*. Write your partner's answer to fill in the blank. The winners are the first pair to finish.

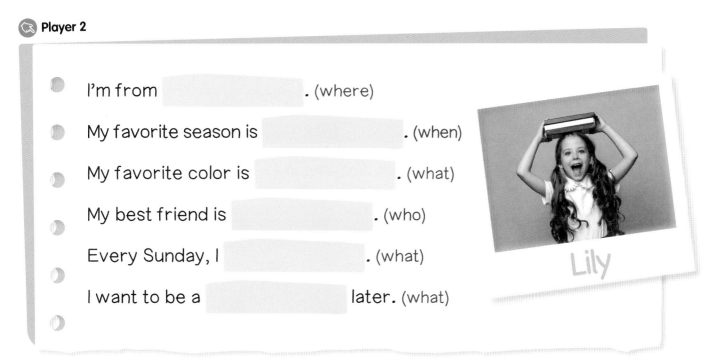

I'm from _____. (where)

My favorite season is _____. (when)

My favorite color is _____. (what)

My best friend is _____. (who)

Every Sunday, I _____. (what)

I want to be a _____ later. (what)

Lily

I'm from Canada.

My birthday is July 1.

My favorite food is pizza.

My favorite singer is Nina.

Every Saturday, I play basketball.

I want to be a police officer later.

Jake

Talk to Me

2ND Edition

Talk to Me

Workbook

3

Happy House

Talk to Me 3

2ND Edition

Workbook

Happy House

Picture Description

Picture Discussion

Talk to Me 3

Story Making

Debate

That Doesn't Belong

A Write the correct words for the pictures.

> flower   vegetables   sheep   wheel   pig   animals

1

_____

2

_____

3

_____

4

_____

5

_____

6

_____

B Look and write.

1

Q Which one is different?

A The s_____ is different. It is a fruit.

2

Q Which one is different?

A The n_____ 5 is different. The others are letters.

C Unscramble and write the sentences.

1  see a horse, / I can / a car, / and a bus.

_____

2  The bird / two legs. / has

_____

D Complete the sentences using the words in the box.

| paper   snake   float   brick |

1 ❶: The _____ is different.
   The others have wings and they can fly.

2 ❷: The _____ is different.
   We can write with a pencil, a colored pencil, and a crayon.

3 ❸: The _____ is different.
   The others _____ on water.

Unit 02 This Is Heavier

A Write the correct words for the pictures.

longer   heavier   vampire   thinner   slower   ghost

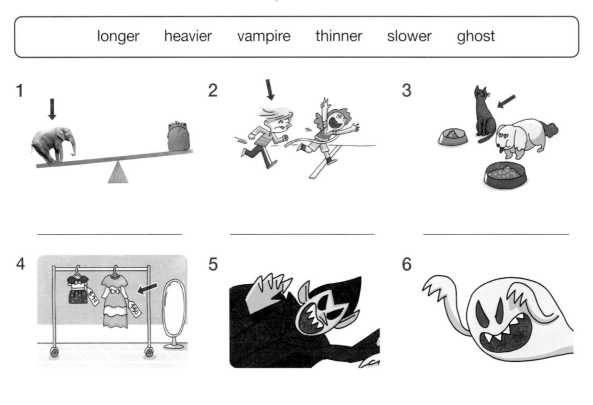

1 _____

2 _____

3 _____

4 _____

5 _____

6 _____

B Look and write.

1

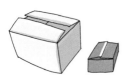

Q Which one is smaller?

A The g_____ box is smaller.

2

Q Who is faster?

A The g_____ is faster.

C Read and match.

Which is heavier, the balloon or the backpack?

The movie theater and the shopping mall are louder than the library.

What other places are louder than the library?

The backpack is heavier than the balloon.

Which dress is more expensive?

The blue dress is more expensive.

D Complete the sentences using the words in the box.

| than   more   scarier |

1 ❶: The girl thinks a ghost is _____ than a vampire.

2 ❷: The boy thinks playing baseball is _____ exciting _____ watching baseball.

Who Is the Youngest?

A Write the correct words for the pictures.

> the biggest   panda   the youngest   the tallest   drawing   zoo

1

_____

2

_____

3

_____

4

_____

5

_____

6

_____

B Look and write.

1

Q What do you want to be the best at?

A I want to be the best at s_____.

2

Q What do you want to be the best at?

A I want to be the best at d_____.

C Unscramble and write the sentences.

1

The grandfather / the oldest. / is

_____

2

is / The alligator / the most dangerous.

_____

D Complete the sentences using the words in the box.

| happy   sad   gifts   sick |

1 ❶: The boy has many birthday _____.
   He feels _____.

2 ❷: The girl wants to go on a picnic.
   But she is _____. She feels _____.

 **Unit 04** The Light Is on in the House

A Write the correct words for the pictures.

> curtain   fly   river   mountain   flag   big balloons

1

_____

2

_____

3

_____

4

_____

5

_____

6

_____

B Look and write.

1

Q What does the place look like?

A There are lots of b_____.

2

Q What does the place look like?

A Some people are riding c_____.

10

C Read and match.

What is the astronaut doing? •

• It looks like it might rain.

What is the weather like? •

• He is floating in space.

D Look and write T for true or F for false.

1 The mom and the daughter are sleeping. (　)

2 There is a brown teddy bear on the bed. (　)

3 I see a tall lamp beside the bed. (　)

That's Not Right!

A Write the correct words for the pictures.

firefighter	nurse	computer	cheetah	skateboard	clown

1

_____

2

_____

3

_____

4

_____

5

_____

6

_____

B Look and write.

1

Q What is wrong with the picture?

A The man is s_____ at the beach.

2

Q What is wrong with the picture?

A The girl is wearing a c_____ on a hot day.

C Unscramble and write the sentences.

1

There is / in the kitchen. / a bed

_____

2

a man in a boat / There is / on the street.

_____

D Complete the sentences using the words in the box.

standing   tent   guitar

1 ❶: There is a _____ in the office.

2 ❷: A woman is playing the _____ in the office.

3 ❸: A man is _____ on the desk.

Unit 06 What Is Similar and Different?

A Write the correct words for the pictures.

> cow   angry   sports uniform   leaves   feed   blossom

1

_____

2

_____

3

_____

4

_____

5

_____

6

_____

B Look and write.

1

Q What is similar about the people?

A They are eating bread and drinking o_____ juice.

2

Q What differences can you find?

A The window on the left is big, but the window on the right is s_____.

C Read and match.

> What are the people doing?

•   •

> They are having a class.

> What is similar about the houses?

•   •

> The roofs look like triangles.

D Look and write T for true or F for false.

1 The girl is wearing red boots. ( )

2 The children are buying ice cream. ( )

3 The children are each holding a book. ( )

Unit 07 How Often Do You Eat Out?

A Write the correct words for the pictures.

> parents   train   airplane   park   order   once a week

1

_____

2

_____

3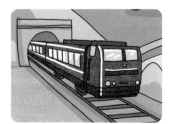

_____

4

	SUN	
(MON)	TUE	WED
THU	FRI	SAT

_____

5

_____

6

_____

B Look and write.

1

Q How often do you do this activity?

A I s_____ English three times a week.

2

Q How often do you do this activity?

A I r_____ a book every day.

16

C Unscramble and write the sentences.

1

never / I / fast food. / eat

_____

2

the movie theater? / do you / How often / go to

_____

D Complete the sentences using the words in the box.

| borrow | dentist | week |

1 ❶: I go to the _____ once a year.

2 ❷: I go to the supermarket once a _____ with my mom.

3 ❸: I go to the library twice a week. I _____ some books.

Unit 08 — What Is He Going to Do?

A Write the correct words for the pictures.

> is going to bake   banana peel   is going to rain   paintbrush   bread   water

1

_____

2

_____

3

_____

4

_____

5

_____

6

_____

B Look and write.

1

Q What is she going to do next?

A She is going to b_____ her teeth.

2

Q What is he going to do next?

A He is going to send the l_____.

C Read and match.

What is he going to do next?

I think her shopping bag is going to break.

What is going to happen to the woman's shopping bag?

He is going to play basketball.

D Look and write T for true or F for false.

1 ❶: He is going to make a snowman. (   )

2 ❷: She is going to skate. (   )

3 ❸: She is going to fall down. (   )

A Write the correct words for the pictures.

helmet   alarm clock   supermarket   sleepy   tired   shorts

1

_____

2

_____

3

_____

4

_____

5

_____

6

_____

B Look and write.

1

Q When do you go to this place?

A I go to the p_____ o_____ when I send Christmas cards.

2

Q When do you go to this place?

A I go to the b_____ when I buy books.

C Unscramble and write the sentences.

1

yawn / when I'm tired. / I

_____

2

The girl / the plants. / is watering

_____

D Complete the sentences using the words in the box.

snowing   gift   thank you

1 The boy is giving a Christmas _____ to the girl.

2 It is _____ outside.

3 I say "_____" when someone helps me.

Let's Make Plans!

A Write the correct words for the pictures.

board game   lunch box   Friday   museum   4 o'clock   baseball stadium

1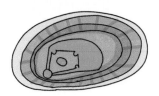

2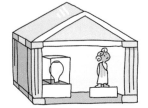

3

_____

_____

_____

4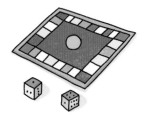

5

6

_____

_____

_____

B Look and write.

1

Q Where will you go this weekend?

A I'll go to the a_____.

2

Q How will you get there?

A I'll t_____ the bus.

C Read and match.

What will the boy do with his money? •

• They will go to the farm in May.

When will the children go to the farm? •

• He will buy a skateboard.

D Look and write T for true or F for false.

1 They will go to the zoo. ( )

2 They will go on Saturday. ( )

3 They will need lunch boxes. ( )

Unit 11 I Would Do If I Could Do

A Write the correct words for the pictures.

| teacher | chef | rocket | kangaroo | race car driver | Halloween |

1

_____

2

_____

3

_____

4

_____

5

_____

6

_____

B Look and write.

1

Q Which job would you choose? Why?

A I would be an a_____ because I want to be famous.

2

Q Which job would you choose? Why?

A I would be a v_____ because I like animals.

C Unscramble and write the sentences.

1  would swim / I / at the beach.

_____

2 He / the room. / is painting

_____

D Complete the sentences using the words in the box.

```
igloos    ice    seals
```

1 ❶: I see _____ and snow.

2 ❷: I see _____ .

3 ❸: I see penguins and _____ too.

Unit 12 We Had a Good Time

A Write the correct words for the pictures.

write a card	have a haircut	celebrate	scared	laugh	have a cold

1 _____

2 _____

3 _____

4 _____

5 _____

6 _____

B Look and write.

1

Q When did you help someone? What did you do?

A It was yesterday.

I w_____ the dishes with Mom.

2

Q When did you help someone? What did you do?

A Last week, I helped an old woman.

I c_____ her heavy bag.

C Read and match.

When was the last time you went to a restaurant?   •

•   They are shopping.

What are the people doing?   •

•   Last week, I went to an Italian restaurant for my mom's birthday.

D Look and write T for true or F for false.

1 The girl and the boy are in the classroom. (   )

2 The girl is looking out the window. (   )

3 The girl looks sad and the boy looks happy. (   )

Ask Me a Question!

A Write the correct words for the pictures.

| bathroom | socks | pumpkin | school | banana | go to bed |

1

_____

2

_____

3

_____

4

_____

5

_____

6

_____

B Look and write.

1

Q W_____ do you do that?

A I take a shower at night.

2

Q W_____ is the girl?

A She is in the hospital.

C Unscramble and write the sentences.

1  eat dinner / at 6:30. / I

_____

2 is bathing / She / the dog.

_____

D Complete the sentences using the words in the box.

| Where | spoon | bread |

1 ❶ _____ : What do you eat soup with?

2 ❷ nest: _____ do birds live?

3 ❸ bakery: Where can you buy _____ ?

Tell Me a Story!

A Write the correct words for the pictures.

> race   fell asleep   wind   turtle   king   visit

1

_____

2

_____

3

_____

4

_____

5

_____

6

_____

B Match the pictures with the correct sentences.

1

•   •   The girl followed the rabbit.

2

•   •   The girl saw a rabbit. It had a watch.

3

•   •   The girl became smaller than the butterfly.

C **Match the number in the picture to the correct sentence.**

1 _____ Country Mouse goes back to the country.

2 _____ A cat chases them and they run away.

3 _____ They have a lot of food.

4 _____ City Mouse invites Country Mouse to the city.

D **Look and write.**

make laughed smart coat

There was once a king. A man came to visit the king and showed him a

_____ . The man said, "Only very smart people can see this beautiful

coat." The king could not see the coat, but he wanted to be _____ .

He said, "Oh, my! It is wonderful. Please _____ me some clothes."

The man came back another day with the king's new clothes.

The king could not see the clothes, but he put them on and then walked

in a parade. A boy called out, "Look, the king has no clothes on!"

Everyone _____ at the king.

Unit 15 — What Do You Think?

A Write the correct words for the pictures.

| going hiking | sister | wake up early | debate | dangerous | pet |

1

2

3

4

5

6

_____ _____ _____

B Look and write.

1

Q I think b_____ j_____ is dangerous.
Do you agree?

A Yes, I think so.

2

Q I think s_____ d_____ is dangerous.
Do you agree?

A No, I don't think so.

C Unscramble and write the sentences.

1

good. / Going to bed / is / early

_____

2

Being a celebrity / good. / would be

_____

D Complete the sentences using the words in the box.

| zoo   good   free |

1 ❶: The giraffes are _____. It looks like Africa.

2 ❷: The giraffes are in the _____.

3 I think zoos are _____ for animals because they are safe there.

Unit 16 What Should Children Do?

A Write the correct words for the pictures.

chores at home   junk food   play sports   play outside   opinions   brainstorm

1

YES   MAYBE   NO

_____

2

_____

3

_____

4

_____

5

_____

6

_____

B Look and write.

1

Q I think children should j_____ r_____

every day. Do you agree?

A Yes, I agree.

2

Q I think children should eat v_____s every day.

Do you agree?

A No, I don't agree.

34

C Read and match.

> Children should play outside every day. What do you think?

> I think children should have cellphones.

> Do you think children should have cellphones?

> I agree because they can get fresh air.

D Complete the sentences using the words in the box.

| should | buying | girl |

1 ❶: One mom is _____ a cellphone for the boy.

2 ❷: One mom isn't buying a cellphone for the _____.

3 I think children _____ not have cellphones.
I want to play outside but they play games on it.

Key Sentences Review

Look and write.

1 (1)

Q Which one is different?

A The s_____ is different. It is a fruit.

(2)

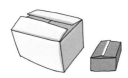

Q Which one is different?

A The n_____ 5 is different. The others are letters.

2 (1)

Q Which one is smaller?

A The g_____ box is smaller.

(2)

Q Who is faster?

A The g_____ is faster.

3 (1)

Q What do you want to be the best at?

A I want to be the best at s_____.

(2)

Q What do you want to be the best at?

A I want to be the best at d_____.

4 (1)

Q What does the place look like?

A There are lots of b_____.

(2)

Q What does the place look like?

A Some people are riding c_____.

5 (1)

Q What is wrong with the picture?

A The man is s_____ at the beach.

(2)

Q What is wrong with the picture?

A The girl is wearing a c_____ on a hot day.

6 (1)

Q What is similar about the people?

A They are eating bread and drinking o_____ juice.

(2)

Q What differences can you find?

A The window on the left is big, but the window on the right is s_____.

7 (1)

Q How often do you do this activity?

A I s_____ English three times a week.

(2)

Q How often do you do this activity?

A I r_____ a book every day.

8 (1)

Q What is she going to do next?

A She is going to b_____ her teeth.

(2)

Q What is he going to do next?

A He is going to send the l_____.

9 (1)

Q When do you go to this place?

A I go to the p_____ o_____ when I send Christmas cards.

(2)

Q When do you go to this place?

A I go to the b_____ when I buy books.

10 (1)

Q Where will you go this weekend?

A I'll go to the a_____.

(2)

Q How will you get there?

A I'll t_____ the bus.

11 (1)

Q Which job would you choose? Why?

A I would be an a_____ because I want to be famous.

(2)

Q Which job would you choose? Why?

A I would be a v_____ because I like animals.

12 (1)

Q When did you help someone? What did you do?

A It was yesterday.
I w_____ the dishes with Mom.

(2)

Q When did you help someone? What did you do?

A Last week, I helped an old woman.
I c_____ her heavy bag.

13 (1)

Q W_____ do you do that?

A I take a shower at night.

(2)

Q W_____ is the girl?

A She is in the hospital.

14 (1)

Q I think b_____ j_____ is dangerous. Do you agree?

A Yes, I think so.

(2)

Q I think s_____ d_____ is dangerous. Do you agree?

A No, I don't think so.

15 (1)

Q I think children should j_____ r_____ every day. Do you agree?

A Yes, I agree.

(2)

Q I think children should eat v_____s every day. Do you agree?

A No, I don't agree.

Talk to Me 3

2ND Edition

Workbook

◆ Components ◆
Student Book / Workbook

◆ Online Resources ◆
eBook, Audio Files, Lesson Plan, Answer Key, Word List,
Test Sheets, PPTs, and others